The Quiet Rage

An Anthology of Polemic Poetry and Stories

By Arika Bhatia

Author's Note

The Quiet Rage began when my father, Mr. Himanshu Bhatia and my brother Mr.Kshiraj Bhatia, told me that I should write a book and I did not think much of it. In the middle of the day, he described how he found my writing skills to be quite commendable— and randomly suggested that maybe I should write a book. The seed of this idea sprouted into a full-fledged branch when my mother, Mrs. Silky Ajmani Bhatia, decided to take this forward and collaborated with me to write this book. Then, I was guided by my mentor, Ms. Shalini Gulyani and Ms. Praniti Gulyani who scattered the sunshine of guidance and support over this project. Combined with the jovial assistance of my best friend, Ms. Samaira Jain, this book became a fully grown tree with the fruits of my hard work on every branch.

I'm fortunate to live in a country as diverse and culturally spread-out as India. Irrespective of its positive homeland does have its share of problems that need to be addressed. In the musty alleys and the shadowy slums, there are several stories that need to be told, and through *The Quiet Rage*, I strive to give these stories a voice and identity. For example, the idea of poverty had disturbed me— whether it was the idea of homelessness or unsanitary areas for the less fortunate. As I began researching social issues in India, I came across issues that I had never heard of like witchcraft acquisition of women which was a bit confusing as I had never come across such bizarre issues.

The idea of poverty had disturbed me whether it was the idea of homelessness or unsanitary areas for the less fortunate. I had always believed that one is the same to another , no being is different. During the creation of these poems I quickly realized this was not the case. And partialness was not the only problem, tons and tons of situations had occurred affecting one's mental physical being which was not ok and never meant to be ok.This journey had taught me that where i am now is a lifestyle that people may have never thought in their dreams i might be grateful but never could be grateful enough.

The Quiet Rage is a collection of personal and self-explanatory poems and emotions. This book aims to explore the untold stories and the open wounds pertaining to social issues in India. I would like to express my deepest gratitude to my mentor, *Ms. Shalini Gulyani*, for her unstoppable support, guidance and dedication. Your endless classes, continuous repetitions, and tireless practice sessions have been invaluable in shaping my journey. As I balanced the challenges of writing with my academic responsibilities, it was your encouragement and patience that truly made a difference. You were not just teachers to me, you were pillars of support who believed in my potential when I struggled to see it myself. Thank you so much for being there every step of the way, for offering your time, knowledge, and, most importantly, your understanding. You gave me the space to nurture my passion for writing, even when it seemed like a mad pursuit amidst everything else. I can never truly express how much your presence in my life has meant, but please know that I carry your lessons with me every day.

Friendships are meant to destress an individual and add joy and laughter to our lives. However, my mate, *Samaira Jain,* stayed by my side as I went about the process of putting this book together. In addition to sitting with me through our writing classes, she also added a spark of laughter and fun to the writing process. We exchanged ideas, shared our writing, and helped each other through the journey. All in all, to everyone who has helped me write the book and ideate each poem, thank you for having me by your side, and for giving me the confidence

From the bottom of my heart, thank you for having me by your side, day after day, and for always giving me the confidence to chase my dreams with relentless dedication.

In Gratitude,

Arika Bhatia

January 2025

Table of Contents

Moving Beyond Magic: A Tribute to the Ragpickers of India

Won the First Position in the Middle School Intra-School Poem Recitation Competition held at Shiv Nadar School, Faridabad from Grade 6th to Grade 8th.

I think I was five, when they told me about a unicorn –
I sat atop a waste-covered rock, drooping and forlorn,
With hollow pits of hunger piercing through my being,
I looked up at the sky – my only known ceiling.

They say that unicorns have magic on their wings,
Magic that can make clouds dance and sing!
However, for me, the clouds only weep –
Through piles of glass and stone, I slowly sweep

Conversations about magic leave me bewildered –
Somersaulting clouds! Singing unicorns! Leave me flustered,
As I set out to pick rags, and clean traffic-covered streets,
With anxiety and worry, I am suddenly replete.

In the evening, my mother cleans rich people's railings –
She is sixty-seven now, old and ailing!

I try my best to make her life easy
Seeing her struggle and strive makes me sick and
queasy!

I wish I could get her the Badi Memsahib's mop,
To the ground, no longer she will have to drop!
However, the money I make goes towards food
Towards clothes and shoes, no matter how crude.

Today, as I push through the plastic and steel
Through piles of vegetable peel, as slippery as a
seal,
I come across a partly bent pink-coloured wiper,
As bright as a rainbow, as sharp as a sniper!

Filled with joy, I bend down and pick up the tool
Without realizing it, I have broken: The Ragpicker's
Rule,
Every object we find must be sent for recycling
Plastic becomes tires used for bicycling.

This evening, I decide to take the mop home
As the sun sets behind the temple's golden dome,
My mother approaches the object with great
trepidation,
Cradling it as though it is her greatest aspiration

There are stars in her eyes, and joy between her
fingers,
Between the wrinkles on her face, the glow of joy
lingers,

This is magic! I realize! This is my unicorn
This essence of joy, my mother's struggles are gone

Neglect Is A Whisper

In the quiet rooms, they sit alone,
Faces marked by years, hearts heavy with silence.
The world has moved on, leaving them behind.
Once, they held the hands of small, bright eyes,
Now they stare at empty spaces, wondering where time has gone.
The rhythm of life quickens, and they can no longer keep pace.
Their stories fade, not with a bang but with a whisper,
Lost in the rush of a world that doesn't stop to look back.

Who will hear their voices now?
Whispers of laughter and sorrow, of hopes and dreams long past.
Who will reach out to hold their hands,
When all they know is the fleeting passage of time?
The chairs at their tables stand empty,
The silence is louder than the noise of the world around them.
They are not invisible, yet they are often ignored,
As if their presence is no longer needed.

But within them is a quiet resilience,
A depth of life lived that cannot be erased by neglect.
They remember the warmth of a touch,

The joy of simple things, and the comfort of love.
They carry a wealth of experience,
Each wrinkle a chapter, each grey hair a story.
Their hearts, though burdened by years, still feel the pulse of the past,
A memory of lives lived fully, even if the world no longer listens.

We rush through our days, consumed by the demands of now,
Forgetting the ones who paved the way for us.
Their wisdom isn't just in the things they say,
But in the way they have endured, the way they have loved.
There is a lesson in every tear they've shed,
A truth in every quiet moment they've lived.
They planted seeds in the gardens of our hearts,
And though the flowers may have faded, the roots remain.

We must not let them fade into the background,
Not let their stories be silenced by time.
For in their silence is a voice that still matters,
A voice that has seen the world in ways we cannot yet understand.
They are not forgotten. They are waiting.
Should not be so quick to turn away.

In their stillness, there is a quiet strength,
A strength that has survived the weight of years.

We owe it to them to listen, to honor,
To show them the same love they gave us without question.
For in remembering them, we remember ourselves,
And in caring for them, we care for the very roots
That will one day support us.

Not out of pity, but with a deep respect
For the lives they have lived and the love they continue to offer,
Even when the world moves too quickly to see.

Echoes of the Silent Trade

In the heat of the day, the market cries,
As tears fall from teary eyes.
Hands bound, but hearts were bound even more,
Sold like cattle to the heartless being.
Whips crack sharp, air turns cold,
Lives are sold, both young and old.
A mother's heart torn apart,
As the chains break what she knew.

Bidders stand with eyes like stone,
Counting lives, which to buy, which to not.
Each price is set, each soul weighed,
In the shadows of the cruel parade.
The auctioneer calls, "What about number eight?"
The bidders say, "No, she's small," "No, worth,"
they say.
With hearts broken, filled with fear,
A child is sold, a man is bought.
Each one marked with a tag,
A price too high for a soul to bear.

Yet in the dark, beneath the pain,
A whisper grows, a quiet strain.
For though they fall, and though they weep,
A strength remains, and it runs deep in the veins.
A spark, though small, refuses to die,
A flicker in the dark, a defiant cry.

In silence that is loud,
A storm brews in the hearts of the bound.

A resilience unseen, but forever there,
A spirit too fierce for the world's cruel glare.
And though their bodies break, their will stands tall,
For they know deep inside—they shall not fall.
And as the chains clink and echo through night,
They hold onto something that no one can fight.

Not the auctioneer, nor the buyers' gaze,
Not the whips, nor the cruelest of days.
For though they part,
They know they never did,
A bond forged in suffering, a love deeply hid.

And in the dark, beneath the stars,
Where pain lingers and hope seems far,
A new dawn rises from broken skin—
A promise that freedom will always begin.
Though they are scattered, though they are torn,
The soul of rebellion is quietly born.
They will rise. And the world will know,
That no chains, no price, can silence that glow.

For in each tear, in each silent cry,
A strength, unbroken, will never die.
Though they part, they are never gone,
A force unyielding, forever drawn.

But there are those who listen, who see the light,
Who rise in the shadows, and stand in the fight.
Their voices join the song, their hearts beat with theirs,
A unity of souls who can no longer bear
To watch the pain, to witness the cost,
For in the silence of the trade, much has been lost.
But they will not forget, not for a second,
For the echoes of those who fell are their own,
And from those echoes, they shall never be alone.

The world may turn its head, may look away,
But their spirits are here, refusing to decay.
For the strength of the fallen is the fuel of the free,
And the chains that once bound them, now hold only a key.
A key to the future, a key to the dawn,
A key that unlocks what the past had withdrawn.

Through every scar, through every fight,
The people who suffer will never lose sight.
They will rise, and they will take their place,
For in the heart of the broken, there's no trace of disgrace.
In the ashes of the auction, a fire burns bright,
An inferno of justice, a beacon of light.

And as the echoes fade, the world will hear,
The voice of the oppressed, ringing clear:
That no matter the cost, no matter the pain,

There will come a time when they break the chain.
For every soul that was sold, every life that was bought,
A reckoning is coming, for all that was lost.

The Place Is The Pain

She is sitting in the back of an overcrowded
ambulance,
The road jerking beneath her,
Each bump is like reminding her that her body is
no longer her own.
The hospital is looming ahead,
Gray and uninviting,
Its walls are a silent proof of neglect in clients.

Her skin is pale,
The veins beneath it darkened and swollen,
But there is no other choice.
The nearest clinic is too far,
Too many miles and hours away,
So she is enduring the pain through journey
To this place,
Where hope is fading,faster than light
Lost in the noise of unspoken sadness.

Inside, the air is thick with sickness,
the scent of medicines for fighting a losing battle.
The floors are sticky, And unsanitary

She is waiting in line,
her legs trembling,
her stomach squeezed in fear,
but the line isn't moving.

A woman in the corner is coughing violently,
the sound echoing off the unstable walls,
while a nurse is hurrying by,
eyes fixed on her clipboard,
never looking up.

The doctor is distant,
his hands swift but cold,
his words clinical,
as if her cancer is just one more case
in an endless stream of sickness
he can never truly see.
She is trying to speak,
but the words are catching in her throat.
Who is listening when the hospital itself is broken?
Who is hearing when pain becomes routine?

Her treatments are delayed,
The equipment is outdated,
Yet she has no choice but to return,
Again and again,
Her hope slipping through her fingers
Like sand blowing in a storm.

Outside, the sun is setting,
But inside the walls, time is standing still.
And she is wondering,
If the cancer inside her is growing,
Or if it is in place.

This hospital,
Slowly, relentlessly,
Eating her alive.
Each visit pulls her deeper,
Until it is not the cancer, but this place that consumes her.

The Veil Of Bacha Posh

In dusty streets where voices fade,

She wears her courage and not her braid.

She walks as though the world were to see

A boy, a man, and yet still never free.

Her eyes, they sparkle, and dreams unfold,

But in her chest is a world that's otherwise told.

She learns how to laugh, to run, to fight,

As she holds back everything feeling too tight.

No room for tears, no need for care.

She climbs and conquers all, unconscious.

But, that in the deep stillness,

Where sorrow should its vigil keep,

The longings of her heart it keeps,

A sister's voice, a mother's hand,

Memories are left in the shifting sand.

For in this bitter game, she's made to play,

A boy today, but a girl someday.

The mask of boyhood is set quickly aside,

A role, a cage, a brief disguise.
When morning comes, and time is right,
What will remain of what was light?
For in the night, when dreams take flight,
She wonders if there's room for light.
Can a girl who's never been a girl
Still find her place in this cruel swirl?
The bacha posh, with hidden pain,
She wears her life as if in vain.
The mask, the act, they intertwine,
Yet in her heart, the stars still shine.
For though the world may never know
Her voice is loud, her spirit glows.
In every step, in every fight,
She's more than just the boy in sight.
One day the mask will fade away,

And in its place, she'll find her way.

A girl, a woman, true and free,

No longer bound by what they decree.

But till that dawn, the bacha posh

Continues on, her heart embossed

With stories untold, with battles won—

The silent war that has just begun.

And though she steps with shadows near,

There's fire within that they won't hear.

Each step she takes, though veiled and small,

Echoes a roar that will never fall.

The world may push, may break, may bind,

But her soul is a tempest, fierce and kind.

For under the mask, beneath the guise,

A girl still dreams with quiet eyes.

And when the time for truth arrives,

She'll step into the light, and thrive.

No more will she hide in dusk,

She will stand as one, both strong and just.

Even in deep silence, though she sleep

Broke,

Her spirit wakes. A woman from hidden dreams

Strongly rising, against the streams

The bacha posh will stand, no more

Behind the mask, behind the door

She'll rise, a proud, free woman—the girl she was,
for all to see.

And in her gaze, the world will know

She is more than what the world bestows.

A heart, a soul, a voice, a mind,

A future yet to be defined.

A Fist Full Of Joy

On Diwali, I held a gift,
A small sum of money wrapped in a beautiful envelope,
A simple offering of the season's joy,
A token of light in a darkened world.
But as I walked through the evening air, with lights flickering in every corner,
A memory began to rise, unbidden and strong,
Of an old woman living in a fragile straw hut,
Her hands frail, her skin almost translucent,
Her eyes were heavy with the weight of a lifetime worn.
She had asked for so little, just a handful of vegetables,
Basic food, nothing more, to ease her hunger,
Her voice barely whispered, as if each word took everything she had.

I could see the deep, quiet resignation in her gaze,
As though she had long learned to live without,
As though she no longer expected to be seen—
Just waiting for some small kindness to relieve her suffering.
In that moment, as I stood there, the wealth in my hands suddenly felt so meaningless,
A mere trinket in a world where a human life could be so fragile.
I wondered how I could walk away while she had

nothing,
How could I, with all I had, ignore her silent plea,
Her dignity hidden beneath the weight of her need?
I turned to my mother, heart heavy with the burden of that moment,
And asked, "Can we bring her what she needs?"
Without a word, my mother understood, her eyes meeting mine,
Her gentle nod said everything I needed to hear.
Together, we returned with food—simple, but heartfelt,
Our hands trembling as we gave it to her,
Her hands shaking as they took it, her face lighting up for just a brief moment,
A quiet gratitude in her eyes, but still that deep emptiness lingering.

We left without speaking, but the silence between us was thick,
Her voice echoing in my mind long after we'd gone—
The weight of a need that couldn't be fixed by mere charity.
That memory stays with me, a quiet grief that hasn't faded,
For in her eyes, I saw the truth I wasn't ready to face:
True wealth isn't in what we possess,
But in what we're willing to share,

In the quiet recognition of suffering,
And the humility to offer what little we have, even if it's not enough.
Now, each Diwali, when the lights glow bright and the fireworks fill the sky,
I think of her, of the woman with the empty hands,
And I remember that the richest gifts are not those we can buy,
But the ones we give freely, with open hearts,
To those whose needs are often unseen,
To those who wait in silence for someone to notice,
Someone to give not just food, but the warmth of compassion,
The light of seeing them, truly seeing them, for the first time.

Victory Against Injustice

In a distant realm, beyond the stars,
A man walked, burdened by his scars.
Grief weighed heavy, his heart torn,
Yet within him, a new hope was born.

A monk arrived, a priest of night,
Fighting for justice, for what was right.
With prayers for the poor, the lost, the weak,
He spoke of peace for those who could not speak.
At dawn, at noon, through endless night,
He battled for those robbed of their light.

For ten long years, he never swayed,
His spirit was strong, though often frayed.
Though the world around him broke and burned,
He pressed on, and his purpose never turned.
His ancestors prayed, "Let your heart change,
Join us in peace, leave sorrow's range."

But the monk persisted, unbent, untamed,
His mission is clear, though never named.
The poor found food, the lost found grace,
Families healed, no longer erased.
Though wealth he never sought, nor fame,
He freed many souls from sorrow's flame.

The man, once bitter, now began to see
That true wealth lies in giving, not in what we keep.

At last, when the monk's work was through,
The man found peace, and his heart grew.
No longer haunted by injustice's night,
He found solace in the monk's endless fight.

For the monk had shown him something deep,
That healing comes from what we give, not seek.
And though his own journey had just begun,
The man understood: the fight must be won,
Not with weapons, nor with might,
But through love, compassion, and light.

The Witch That Never Was

"She brings bad luck," they whispered.
"She's a witch." She they thought

Her husband, once her protector,
Now Looked at her differently
The child fell ill,
"All because of her " the murmured

The fever burning through his small body,
And when he died,
Her husband's eyes grew hard with suspicion.
The villagers agreed,
Her silence, her knowledge of herbs,
Became the signs of dark magic.
"She curses us," they said.
"She must be a witch."

The word spread like wildfire—
Her name no longer spoken with kindness,
But with fear and accusation.
Her every movement was questioned,
Her every gesture is seen as a spell.
The men stood in the square,
Eyes narrowed, fingers pointed,
And soon, the village became certain.
"She is the cause of our suffering."

They came for her one night,
Torches in hand,
Her husband standing silently behind them,
Too afraid to speak.
They tied her to the tree at the village's edge,
Accusing her of cruelty,
Of casting spells

On the land.
She did not resist,
Her heart breaking in silence,
For she had no magic to confess.

As the flames consumed her,
The village believed they had rid themselves of evil.
But when the rains still did not come,
When the crops failed for another season,
They realized the truth too late.
They had not burned a witch,
But a woman whose only crime
Was just being different.
And in the ashes,
The real curse remained
Their fear, their cruelty.
The curse they feared Was their own.

The Flame That Refused to Die

The earth beneath his feet
Cracks open like an old wound,
The weight of it pressing
Against the breath in his chest.
There is no escape,
Only the endless stretch of the horizon,
The unforgiving sun
That watches with cold eyes.

But in the quiet places,
Where no one speaks,
Where no one dares to hope,
There is a flicker —
Small, fragile,
Like a leaf caught in the wind,
But it does not break.

The world asks for everything,
Takes everything,
And yet the heart keeps beating,
Keeps holding on
To a memory,
To a thought
That maybe, just maybe,
There is something more.

The debts pile high,
The land dries out,
But still, the body stands.
Still, the voice rises
Against the storm.

For what is a man
If not the sum of his choices,
The echo of his dreams
Shouting in the dark?
Ram Lal knows the road ahead
Will be long and hard,
But the flame inside him,
Although it is small, it will never die.

He may fall,
But he will rise again,
With quiet strength,
Driven by a promise to himself.
The journey may be uncertain,
But as long as the sun rises,
He will too be.

Life of the Children of Women Prisoners

Mother, I Have Some Questions

Mom, are you there?
Go on, sweetie.

Okay…

Do they pity me?
I just want to touch the grass,
Fly like a bird,
And most of all, I want to be myself.

I live in isolation,
With no one to talk to.
Don't they know I have dreams, too?
Hopes and aspirations—
But these are the only few minutes I have with you.

I don't know when I'll see you again.
Sister's not here; she's with the older kids,
Exposed to things I don't understand,
To words that hurt,
Things I don't want her to see.

Mom, where is Mrs. Stevens?
She's my favorite teacher.
I don't have the help I need,
No support for my schoolwork.

I miss everything—
Your hugs, your care,
The way you kept me safe.
I miss it all, more than you know.

Mom, it's all going to be okay,
Susie from the UN is here with us.
They say children should always be treated in their best interest.
You're going to be safe.

See you later, Mom.
And remember what I said.

1979 Pearl High School Shooting

Forgive me please!
Show mercy! Please let me go
Officer, "I will not till you tell the truth"
I didn't do anything I am harmless
Well! The school's Assistant Principal,
Joel Myrick says otherwise
Officer, "The trial has started"
If you give up the right to remain silent,
Anything you say
Or do can and will be used against you in a court of law"
Officer"well your first criminal offence
To the law started by fatally stabbed and bludgeoning your mother,
Mary Ann Woodham,
As she prepared for a morning jog"
Officer " is that true Mr woodham"
Absolutely i can't remember killing my mother
What a kind soul she was
Officer" another offence,
Young man lying to police that comes in 182.
False information, with intent to cause public servant to use his lawful power
To the injury of another person
Officer "despite we will move on ,
Would you like to share your crime
That you committed further on that day"

Luke Woodham takes a sigh relieving his anger
And says fine
I then drove his mother's Toyota Tercel to Pearl High School.
Wearing a trench coat to conceal the rifle
I was carrying
Officer" a dangerous weapon ,isn't it ?"
Then entered the school and gave a manifesto
To Justin Sledge.
Officer "Sledge, realising what was about to occur,
Gathered some friends and hid in the safety of the library
While the shooting took place,
Mhhh now it all makes sense"
Officer " hey officer mice can you bring the student".
Commons with classmate Justin Sledge
When Woodham walked up and spoke to Sledge.
Justin Sledge then told him,
"No matter what I heard, no matter what I saw, don't turn around.
Just keep going forward
I didn't see anything. I just heard gunshots."
Officer "Thank you for coming in you can go now "
Officer well after all that I'll continue,
Mr Woodham then fatally shot Lydia Kaye Dew and Christina Menefee,
His former girlfriend,
Then, went on to wound seven others.

After that school's Assistant Principal,
Joel Myrick, retrieved a .45 calibre semi-automatic
pistol from his truck and,
Spotting Woodham attempting to flee the parking
lot
After the shooting, I shouted for him to stop.
Woodham lost control of his vehicle, and Myrick
ordered him out of the car at gunpoint
And detained him until I arrived at the scene

Where Sky Whispered Promises

Jesingbhai Makwana
Ended his days in silence,
In the fields where crops once flourished,
And the sky whispered promises
That was never seen, never fulfilled.
Now, his wife stands in that same still earth,
Her hands searching for signs of rain,
Her heart echoing with the absence of his laughter—
The laughter of Makwana,
A sound now lost to time.
A quietness has fallen over the land,
The growth has stopped,
And warmth has not touched the soil in years.
She watches the children,
Who will never ask her questions again.

The debts he carried
Have settled on her shoulders,
Invisible but crushing.
The weight of survival
Is heavy in the long, empty hours
When she dreams of a life
That was never meant to be for them.
She remembers his hands in the soil,
The promise of tomorrow
Woven into the furrows he plowed.

But now, all that's left is the barren earth
And the sorrow of unspoken words.

The children, lost in their own fleeting joy,
Search for him in the morning sun,
In the rustle of the leaves,
In the dust of the roads.
They run behind the bushes,
Calling his name,
But he is no longer there,
His absence swallows the world whole.

The crops he once grew,
The soil he tenderly loved,
Have turned bitter,
Wilted in the heat of his departure.
The land, once a promise of plenty,
Now stands as a reminder of everything they've lost.
The fields no longer whisper of hope,
But hum with the silence
That stretches far beyond their reach—
A silence so vast
That no voice can fill it,
No hands can heal it.

In his absence,
There is a wound, deep and raw,
A silence that has carved its place
In the hearts of those left behind.

His family, bound to the earth
He once tended,
Now faces a future uncertain,
A future where each day is a struggle,
And every step feels like walking through fog.
They carry the weight of a loss too profound
For words to grasp,
A grief that lingers in the air,
In the dust,
In the soil they can no longer trust.

The Ghost Of Our Gadgets

In the shadows, where circuits fade,
Lies a forest of metal, a graveyard parade,
Of broken screens and forgotten wires,
Echoing whispers of the pollution's heart.
Once they hummed a tune with life and light,
Told our stories, brought our sights,
Now they lie in silent decay,
A sea of waste, where once they'd swayed.
Tons and tons, they pile and lay,
Choking the earth with fritters away.

Plastic bones and copper veins,
Fingers of the future wrapped in chains—
Chains of e-waste, a modern curse,
A cycle of consumption, for better or worse.
The device once bright, now dimmed and cold,
A future traded for gadgets bold.
The promises of progress, shining new,
Leave behind a trail of toxic residue.
In the landfill's deep and endless mound,
Where dreams of innovation no longer resound,
They cry a silent hum, forgotten and ignored,
A call for renewal, but unheard, deplored.

And yet, we crave the next in line,
Another upgrade, another sign,
To leave behind the old and worn,
Ignoring the legacy they've borne.

How many times will we discard,
A piece of history, a thing once starred?
Each device a story, a fleeting spark,
Now lost within the dark,
Replaced too quickly, without a thought,
For the life it led, the value it brought.

So let us pause, and gently sigh,
As we watch our technology die,
And ponder the cost before we race,
To discard again in this ceaseless chase.
How many ghosts shall we create,
As we march on toward a future too late?
The ones we've loved, the ones we've used,
Cast aside, abused, and refused.
For each discarded screen, each forgotten wire,
A bit of our soul is lost to the fire.

For the ghosts of our gadgets will remain,
Haunting the earth with their silent pain.
In the soil, in the air, in the oceans wide,
Their whispers linger, and cannot hide.
They will remain for times unseen,
In the dirt, in the dust, in the spaces in between.
A future of innovation paved in waste,
A price too high, an irreversible taste.
The technology of now, the promises of bold,
Fading into memories, into stories told.

And as we race toward what comes next,
Let's not forget the toll, the effects.
For in the end, when progress has passed,
The ghosts of our gadgets will last—
A silent reminder, forevermore,
Of what we leave behind, what we ignore.

The Feast Of Gratitude

Reena stood by the door,
hands clasped, watching the scene—
Diwali at the Suris',
marigolds, lanterns, aroma filling the air.
The children, Aditya and Meera,
tossing jalebi, laughing,
while sweets and samosas
were discarded carelessly.
Each bite wasted,
a twist in Reena's heart,
a reminder of her own children
fighting for scraps.
In her home, Diwali meant
simple prayers, dal, roti,
a humble meal shared,
and joy in what little they had.
"Reena, take the sweets away,"
Meera called out,
and Reena, hands trembling,
gathered the leftovers—
a warm samosa slipped into her apron.
But then Mrs. Suri's voice:
"Take some food home.
It's Diwali. You deserve it."
Reena froze, then whispered,
"Thank you, ma'am."
Her heart ached with gratitude.

At home, her children's faces
lit up with joy,
as they shared the food,
laughter filling the small room.
This was the best Diwali,
not in abundance,
but in love,
in light,
and in the kindness
that made her feel worthy.
The flicker of diyas danced in their eyes,
and Reena knew, in that humble moment,
that wealth was measured not by what one has,
but by the grace of giving,
and the joy of simple, shared things.
As the night deepened,
the sounds of fireworks echoed in the distance,
but Reena's heart stayed still,
wrapped in the quiet warmth of her family.
She thought of the Suris' glittering feast,
and felt a deeper richness—
for in the smallest acts of kindness,
a person can find more than gold.
The children huddled close,
clutching their samosas,
and in that room,
the light of Diwali burned bright.

To Be A Woman In This World

Life is harder for those who cannot hear,
A world of noise, yet silence wraps around them,
Their voices fade into the hum of indifference,
Misunderstood, invisible, they are unseen.

In spaces where others speak,
They are left to navigate the gaps,
Their words linger in the air,
Unspoken, dismissed, erased.

To be a woman in this world,
And deaf, is to carry two burdens, What is life they wonder
Both the weight of silence
And the weight of being silenced, Is it ?

They are asked to be louder,
To shape themselves to fit a mold
That is not theirs,
A mold that does not listen,
That does not care to hear their truth.

The world shouts, but it forgets
That silence is not weakness,
That not being heard does not erase
The power within them,
The strength in their stillness.

But each day, they rise,
Facing a world that does not understand,
Not because they cannot speak,
But because their voices are not valued,
Because their silence frightens,
Because it challenges what is known.

Still, they move through it all,
With fierce determination,
With hearts that beat loudly,
With minds that think,
And with a power that cannot be quieted.

Life is harder for those who cannot hear,
But they are no less whole,
No less worthy,
No less resilient,
Than anyone who speaks and is heard.

A Ship In A Harbour Is Safe But That Is Not What Ships Are Built For

I am set in the harbour's calm
My cleats untouched my engine never on
I am safe from weather and the terrible winds that roar
for i am old and ailing
I know you want me not to struggle and strive although

A silent desire for fierce is a whizzy dream
For though the port seems kind and motionless,
The soul was born to chase the thrill.

Us , like ships, were built to glide
Not bound to comfort or to home.
The tides of life may surge, may start
But only through the storm, we wake

The harbour's peace may soothe the mind,
But peace alone can leave us blind

What is life with no adventure

Maybe a plane curry with no spice

It would taste bland right
just like our dreams with no light
What would we shout aloud in excitement rather

than ship ahoy

Maybe we our, our owns prison-
Stopping abstract thoughts from day to day life

The harbour whispers " stay don't go" although
The *Titanic*
The *Titanic* sailed with hearts so sure,
A monument built, so strong, *A thought* so pure
An unsinkable ship they roared
Harland and Wolff shipyard said with their heart
our ship has now left the port

A ship may rest in harbour's calm,
Although titanic made water touch
its cleats wet its sails harmed

So let us leave the harbour behind,
And chase the dreams we've yet to find.
For ships are meant for oceans wide,
And we, like them, are meant to float high.

Embers of everything

Arika's Previous Writings

On The Other End Of The Sword

I am perched on the edge of my car with no idea of what the future holds. I just witnessed a village where a girl was watching me with envious eyes. She was holding buckets of water, and was clearly very tired. As the car slowed down, I witnessed the inside of her little hut. Her brothers were sitting on the bed and watching TV. They were clearly having a blast, and all the hard work and toil was being done by the girl. I had always heard about gender discrimination, but this was the first time I was witnessing it so closely.

A black leotard or a strong sword?

My mother's voice interrupted my thoughts. As the car sped up, I was filled with anguish
with no idea about what to do next."Arika, are you sure about this?" asked my mother in a very concerned tone. " I understand that it's never easy to change a sport that you've been playing for more than six years! We can always go back to gymnastics,"she said in an assuring tone.

Just then, I was transported to the day I had to decide between fencing and gymnastics for my school sport. This is when my willpower was tested. As I went back to my gymnastics days, I remember the feeling of pulling off a perfect landing after jumping off the springboard. It's going to stay with me for a lifetime. But this wasn't just about the perfect land, it was about my future sport.

"Mom," I spoke softly. "I don't know, but I will try to figure it out on my own. Whichever path I choose, I'll walk it with everything I have got. I know gymnastics is a sport of flexibility, balance, and coordination. I know a lot of moves like cartwheels, handstands, and whatnot. But now, something inside me is redirecting me towards something else, and that's fencing. A fast-paced, strategic combat sport that demands not only physical agility but also mental sharpness and focus. I have made my final choice and chosen fencing as my sport for day, night and the rest of my life. So, let's dedicate ourselves to it and continue it as my long, lifetime sport! It's something that has taught me much discipline, focus, and perseverance. It has been a place where I learnt to push through physical pain, stop my mental thoughts, and never settle for anything less than my best. It's not only perfecting moves; it is all about anticipating the next move, reading the opponent, and reacting with speed, precision, and strategy. It's both mental and physical. That means it's double the effort, and I'm willing to give it my all,"

3 Years Later

"Mom! Mom!" I called, as I ran to the edge of the indoor stadium. I was anxious to remove my uniform, and was drenched in beads of perspiration.

"Yes, darling, here I come," responded my mother, smiling at me.

"Listen to what happened. I won the first match, then the second, and finally the medal match. The score went from 1 to 2, then 3. It went on till fourteen, but I unfortunately lost by one point,"

"That is ok, darling; think about the people who lost in the first match. You are a winner in my eyes,"

"So let's have a party for my wins, mom!"

" Sure, why not?

As we drove to my favorite restaurant, I stared out the window, lost in thought. After a few moments of silence, I finally asked, "Hey mom, can I ask you something? Am I fortunate?" My mother smiled at me warmly. "Yes, a very fortunate child," she replied, her tone light. "Don't you think a lucky child is one who gets to go to nationals?" But I wasn't asking about that. I rested my head back against the window, thinking carefully before speaking again. "No, mom, not like that. I mean. Is it that I'm too privileged? Some girls don't even get the chance to play sports."

My mother asked in confusion, her brow in a puzzle . "What are you talking about? Isn't your gym teacher letting you play? I'll talk to him myself if that's the case." I shook my head, still still in despair. "No, it's not about that. It's about the girls who grow up in places where they don't have the opportunity. In communities where things don't change, where sports aren't even an option. What about them? Do they just sit at home, never get to experience what I do?" I felt a knot in my heart, struggling with the unfairness of it all, knowing that my privilege could never be their reality

I knew I was fortunate to have the opportunity to play sports, but many underprivileged girls face barriers like discrimination, lack of resources, and societal expectations that can go up to any extent to prevent them from participating. Without access to sports, they miss out on the confidence, teamwork, and life skills that come with it. While I had the privilege to play, I feel it's important to help create opportunities for all girls to experience these benefits!

True Power Of Friendship

A Tribute to my Best Friend Samaira Jain

She and me,
Is the example
I would take for friendship—
Far out or close together,
We stay with each other.
We have magnetic power,
A force that keeps us bound.
One at the north, one at the south,
But always, we stay close,
Our hands still joined.

We started together,
And though the paths may change,
Our hearts remain the same,
For true friendship is never lost,
No matter where life leads.
Even when the seasons shift,
And time takes us in different directions,
The bond stays strong,
Like roots that grow deep in the earth.

We are best friends—
The kind of people who understand
Without needing to speak.
We are each other's world,
And that's why we are "WE"—

Two halves of a whole,
Forever connected.

When Social Justice Got A Magical Twist

News reporter Morse over here.

Twenty-five murder cases all over the United States.
Why all of these murders?
Why in the US?
Why 25?
Why, why, why?
The question is spread in the town, Alaska and its people.
But it isn't just them—New York City, Los Angeles, San Francisco,
Las Vegas, Chicago, Miami, and whatnot!
Although we perch here with one thought in our minds:
What happened to our loved ones?
Well, worry no more!
Detective Morse is here! To solve the crime that no one else can.
Let's get freedom today, tonight, any time, but let's do it!
I held my newly decorated candy cane stick and went off unknown.
My disguise? Huh, don't even talk about it.
Well, it was a middle-aged man wanting to please his children,
So dressed like Santa to get the turkey for dinner.
And not to be surprised, it worked, partially –

Except for the kids accepting gifts from me as they put their arms spread into the wide open air.
But it was now time to figure out the culprits of this year's Christmas madness.

The Grinch was top priority by the town, although it isn't up for them to prove or decide.
The duty is all on me and only me.
Up the hills I went, down the valleys I go.
No trace of green fur throughout the borders of Alaska.
But little did I know what those long lines meant.
I traveled my way to the mountain where Grinch lives.
I had to know my guess was a miss.
I didn't, though, so I went further.

I got to know I was wrong.
A question cracked in my head:
Is Krampus the mastermind behind the crime?
I was flabbergasted at my foolish mistake.
Those long lines were his nails.
I scratched my head, pondering how I was going to catch the monster.
An evil thought occurred:
I was wondering, would it be absurd if
I was the new Krampus taking his role?

In this town, detective work is the only job to have.
But women aren't allowed to do it.

It’s a man’s world here, and any woman who dares to try—
She’s setting herself up for failure.
But I’m here, fighting the system, solving the case.

So I put on a body suit, covered it with black feathers,
And the long nails from last Halloween came to work.
With a little fixing with my hand, I made it go as planned.
I went to St. Nicholas, and said, “May I be the Krampus of the holiday?”
“I’ll be the best one yet.”
Yes! I got the job and the location of the gruesome Krampus.
So I evict him from his job of taking heartfelt humans.
It will be better if I go now or the truth may never come out.
Hello, old Krampus, you may leave now. No worth of growling.
I’m in charge now, ha ha.
Where are the children? Tell me now or I will kick you out—
Not from your job, out of the world.
Krampus said, “Yes, master.”
Perfect as I planned, now just have to take those whimpering kids

And fly away from the North Pole.
Mission three hundred and one successful.

But there's something you should know.
These murders weren't just random acts of violence—they were the cry of the forgotten.
The people pushed aside by society, abandoned and ignored.
They don't celebrate the holidays. They don't fit in with the festivities.

Arion myth with a twist

The musician of hearts, the musician of love, the musician of peace
Arion, a renowned artist from the lands of Leboses, had become a crowd pleaser by not just being a musician but a great scientist
The mystic voice of his singing reverberated through the land of Greece
It stopped cyclones, finished wars, and calmed the stormiest seas
This magic finally left the land
Venturing to the world of music
Arion sang until he couldn't
Studied until the end of time
He climbed mountains to reach from a land to another
He fought army
Conquered police to sing one song
That one song was worth more than what he does
That one song was worth more than money
A song that a trillionaire can not buy let alone a millionaire
Countries with beaches beheld the most alluring dolphins and seahorses
They beheld sea creatures like no other
In Hawaii, the last tour
He looked at a mollusk, nudibranchs, and leafy seadragon

All more beautiful than ever
But other than the beauty, Arion saw the scars of the world:
The oceans dying, the beaches fading, the creatures endangered.
His heart ached as he saw how greed for resources tore through the lands he once serenaded.
The very ecosystems that inspired his songs were now on the brink of collapse—
Torn apart by pollution, overfishing, and climate change,
Ignored by those with power who cared only for wealth, not the soul of the earth.
At last, his tour was over
He hopped on a ship with fellow mates from his tours
However, the ship's crew was not exactly honest
They stared with jealousy at Arion's jewels
Almost like they were pondering a plan
A plan to kill someone
Arion knew this was going to happen
He begged the crew to sing one last time
The foolish men thought no more
And enjoyed a delight while seeing the man's last performance
As soon as the song was over
Arion leaped like an adroit ballerina into the ocean
But his story was not over yet
The music that he played lured a Flying Gurnard

It called its family and made sure that Arion went
home safely
The countries that he toured in now did not only
make a statue of him
But also added the infamous Flying Gurnard and his
beloved guitar
And though the world celebrated Arion's life,
It was his message, woven into every note, that
persisted:
To protect what is beautiful,
To hear the cries of the earth,
And to never let the music fade in the face of greed.

www.ingramcontent.com/pod-product-compliance
Lightning Source LLC
LaVergne TN
LVHW090129160826
845673LV00015B/1128

* 9 7 9 8 8 9 6 9 9 2 0 9 7 *